GOAT: Women in Sports

Lindsey Vonn

Skiing GOAT

HOT TOPICS

Gareth Stevens Publishing

By Kristen Rajczak Nelson

Please visit our website, www.garethstevens.com. For a free color catalog of all our high-quality books, call toll free 1-800-542-2595 or fax 1-877-542-2596.

Library of Congress Cataloging-in-Publication Data
Names: Rajczak Nelson, Kristen, author.
Title: Lindsey Vonn : skiing goat / skiing GOAT / Kristen Rajczak Nelson.
Description: Buffalo, New York : Gareth Stevens Publishing, 2025. | Series: GOAT. Women in sports | Includes bibliographical references and index.
Identifiers: LCCN 2023033100 | ISBN 9781538293713 (library binding) | ISBN 9781538293706 (paperback) | ISBN 9781538293720 (ebook)
Subjects: LCSH: Vonn, Lindsey–Juvenile literature. | Skiers–United States–Biography–Juvenile literature.
Classification: LCC GV854.2.V66 R35 2025 | DDC 796.93092 [B]–dc23/eng/20230721
LC record available at https://lccn.loc.gov/2023033100

First Edition

Published in 2025 by
Gareth Stevens Publishing
2544 Clinton St
Buffalo, NY 14224

Designer: Leslie Taylor
Editor: Kristen Rajczak Nelson

Photo credits: Cover (photo) B.Stefanov/Shutterstock.com, (wreath) Igoron_vector_3D_render/Shutterstock.com, (banner, cover & series background) RETHELD DESIGN IRI/Shutterstock.com, (skiing icon) popicon/Shutterstockcom; pp. 5, 19 B.Stefanov/Shutterstock.com; pp. 7, 25 Featureflash Photo Agency/Shutterstock.com; p. 9 Hans Christiansson/Shutterstock.com; p. 11 Mangoman88/https://commons.wikimedia.org/wiki/File:2002_Winter_Olympics_-_Countdown_Clock_-_5_September_2012.jpg; p. 13 Arthur Mouratidis/https://commons.wikimedia.org/wiki/File:Lindsey_Kildow_Aspen.jpg; p. 15 Gerwig Loffelholz/https://commons.wikimedia.org/wiki/File:Vonn-lindsey_08-03-08_-_008.jpg; p. 17 Duncan Rawlinson/ https://commons.wikimedia.org/wiki/File:Women%27s_Super_G_podium_at_Whistler_Creekside_closeup.jpg; pp. 21, 23 PHOTOMDP/Shutterstock.com; p. 27 PACIFIC PRESS/Alamy.com; p. 29 Tinseltown/Shutterstock.com.

Printed in the United States of America

Some of the images in this book illustrate individuals who are models. The depictions do not imply actual situations or events.

CPSIA compliance information: Batch #CSGS25: For further information contact Gareth Stevens, New York, New York at 1-800-542-2595.

Contents

Comeback Queen

Lindsey Vonn could be called the GOAT—greatest of all time—in **Alpine** skiing just on her record alone. But she also faced many **injuries** only to come back and keep winning. Her success is **inspirational** as well as notable!

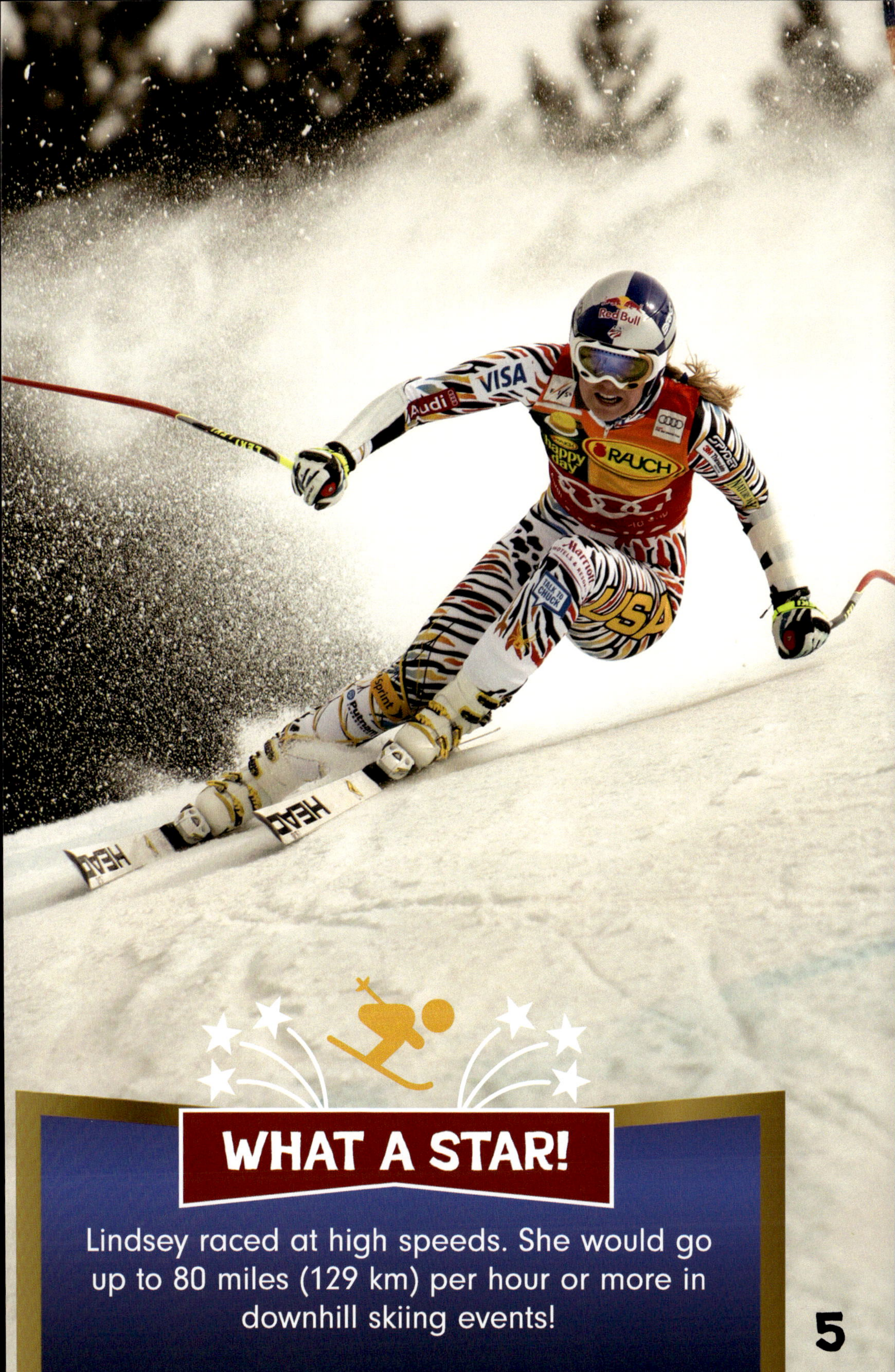

WHAT A STAR!

Lindsey raced at high speeds. She would go up to 80 miles (129 km) per hour or more in downhill skiing events!

Family Sport

Lindsey was born Lindsey Kildow on October 18, 1984, in Minnesota. She grew up with two younger sisters and two younger brothers. Lindsey's dad, Alan, was a ski racer when he was younger. He first took her skiing when she was about 2 years old!

LINDSEY (RIGHT) WITH HER SISTER KARIN KILDOW

WHAT A STAR!

Lindsey's family moved to Vail, Colorado, when she was 11. Vail is known for great skiing!

Racing for a Dream

Lindsey raced for the first time at age 7. When she was 9, she met her hero, Olympic skier Picabo Street. Picabo told Lindsey to keep following her dreams! Lindsey did—and won her first **international** race at age 14.

WHAT A STAR!

Lindsey tells those who have a dream "to work hard when the likelihood of success is not high. Because it's something you want to do."

Young Olympian

Lindsey started skiing **professionally** around 2000. She did well enough in her races to be chosen for the USA ski team. At just 17, she got sixth place in the Alpine combined at the 2002 Winter Olympics in Salt Lake City, Utah! The combined includes both a downhill and **slalom** run.

WHAT A STAR!

After skiing well in the Olympics, Lindsey was told to go back to lower-level races. It was a letdown, but it just made Lindsey work harder!

By the 2006 Olympics, Lindsey was one of the top Alpine skiers in the world. However, she had a bad crash on a training run. Lindsey was well enough to race in four Olympic events, but she didn't **medal** in any of them.

WHAT A STAR!

Lindsey earned the U.S. Olympic Spirit Award at the 2006 Olympics for her bravery in returning to the games after the crash.

The Top of the Mountain

Lindsey had another injury in 2007. But she came back and won her first World Cup title! She also won her 10th World Cup downhill race, breaking the American record of most downhill World Cup wins, held in part by Picabo Street.

WHAT A STAR!

Lindsey married another professional skier, Thomas Vonn, in 2007. They ended their marriage in 2013.

Lindsey made history at the 2010 Winter Olympics. She was the first American woman to ever win the downhill! She beat the next skier by more than half a second. Lindsey also won a bronze medal in the super giant slalom, or super-G.

2010 OLYMPICS

WHAT A STAR!

Lindsey won a lot of races—but she also missed finishing many races. Skiing as fast and fearlessly as Lindsey did means crashing too.

Lindsey continued to win. She won the women's overall World Cup title in 2008, 2009, 2010, and 2012! Additionally, Lindsey won two gold medals at the World Championships in 2009, as well as a silver in the downhill in 2011.

WORLD CUP, 2012

WHAT A STAR!

By winning in 2008 and 2009, Lindsey was the first American woman to win back-to-back overall World Cup titles.

Ups and Downs

In 2013, Lindsey faced her worst injuries yet. She crashed during the super-G at the World Championships. While Lindsey made it back to racing by the end of the year, she soon got hurt again. Because of this, Lindsey wasn't part of the 2014 Olympics.

WHAT A STAR!

When Lindsey returned to racing in 2015, she broke the record for most World Cup race wins by a female Alpine skier. She held this record until 2023 when Mikaela Shiffrin broke it.

Lindsey became the winningest downhill Alpine skier of all time—man or woman—in 2016. She won the World Cup downhill title that year too. Then she broke her arm. More injuries followed in 2017 and 2018.

WHAT A STAR!

Skiing is an **individual** sport. Lindsey told *Sports Illustrated*: "No matter who it is out there, when you're ski racing, you're skiing by yourself. There's no one holding your hand through it."

One Last Olympics

Lindsey worked hard to keep racing, and she made it to the 2018 Olympics in South Korea. Lindsey brought home a bronze medal in the downhill. But she was starting to question how much more her body could take.

WHAT A STAR!

Lindsey has depression, a condition in which feelings of sadness and hopelessness make it hard to go through everyday life. She has said: "I think mental health, you train it like you do any other muscle in your body."

Retirement

Lindsey raced for the last time at the 2019 World Championships. She won a bronze medal in the downhill! When she **retired** afterward, she had 82 Alpine skiing World Cup wins, just five away from breaking the record for the most of any skier.

LINDSEY'S LAST RACE, 2019

WHAT A STAR!

One thing Lindsey wanted to do before she retired didn't happen. She wanted to race against male skiers!

Since retiring, Lindsey has hosted a TV show, put out ski gear lines, and even driven racecars! She hasn't stopped skiing altogether either. In 2023, Lindsey skied one of the world's hardest downhill courses in Austria!

WHAT A STAR!

Lindsey wants to help girls in sports. The Lindsey Vonn Foundation hosts camps and gives out scholarships, or money that helps girls pay for school or sports training.

Lindsey Vonn BY THE NUMBERS

Olympic Medals: 3

Olympic Games Participated in: 4

World Championship Medals: 7

World Cup Race Wins: 82

World Cup Overall Titles: 4

Other World Cup Titles:

Downhill: 8
Super-G: 5
Combined: 3

Years as a Professional Skier: 18

For More Information

BOOKS

Bolte, Mari. *Mikaela Shiffrin: Olympic Skiing Legend.* North Mankato, MN: Capstone Press, 2024.

Nieson, Joan. *Girl Athlete: Powerful Stories from Game-Changing Women.* New York, NY: Downtown Books, 2021.

WEBSITES

Lindsey Vonn
www.teamusa.org/us-ski-and-snowboard/athletes/lindsey-vonn
Review Lindsey's Olympic career on her Team USA page.

Lindsey Vonn Official Website
www.lindseyvonn.com/en/home/
Follow everything Lindsey is doing on her website.

Publisher's note to educators and parents: Our editors have carefully reviewed these websites to ensure that they are suitable for students. Many websites change frequently, however, and we cannot guarantee that a site's future contents will continue to meet our high standards of quality and educational value. Be advised that students should be closely supervised whenever they access the internet.

Glossary

Alpine: Having to do with being high in the mountains, in particular the Alps.

individual: Having to do with just one member of a group.

injury: Harm or damage done to the body.

inspirational: Causing someone to want to do or make something.

international: Involving two or more countries.

medal: To win first, second, or third place in an event. Also, a prize given to the winners of a competition. They are often made of metal and worn on a ribbon around the neck.

professional: Earning money from an activity that many people do for fun.

retire: For athletes, to stop taking part in a sport professionally.

slalom: A skiing race on a course with many turns that are marked by flags.

Index